World of Reptiles

Gila Monsters

by Jason Glaser

Consultants:
The Staff of the Reptile Gardens
Rapid City, South Dakota

Capstone press

Mankato, Minnesota

Bridgestone Books are published by Capstone Press,
151 Good Counsel Drive, P.O. Box 669, Mankato, Minnesota 56002.
www.capstonepress.com

Library of Congress Cataloging-in-Publication Data
Glaser, Jason.
    Gila monsters / Jason Glaser.
        p. cm.—(Bridgestone books. World of reptiles)
    Summary: "A brief introduction to Gila monsters, discussing their characteristics, range,
habitat, food, reproduction, offspring, and dangers. Includes a range map, life cycle diagram,
and amazing facts"—Provided by publisher.
    Includes bibliographical references and index.
    ISBN-13: 978-0-7368-5424-5 (hardcover)
    ISBN-10: 0-7368-5424-X (hardcover)
    1. Gila monster—Juvenile literature. I. Title. II. Series.
QL666.L247G53 2006
597.95'952—dc22   2005015244

Editorial Credits
Becky Viaene, editor; Enoch Peterson, set designer; Patrick D. Dentinger and Kim Brown,
    book designers; Jo Miller, photo researcher; Scott Thoms, photo editor; Tami Collins, life cycle
    illustrator; Nancy Steers, map illustrator

Photo Credits
Bruce Coleman Inc./Jeff Foott, 10; John Hoffman, 18; Tom Brakefield, 12
David Liebman Nature Photography/Dennis Sheridan, 1, 4; Gila Ranch/Chris Reimann, 6, 16;
    Roger Rageot, 20
Visuals Unlimited/Joe & Mary Ann McDonald, cover

1 2 3 4 5 6 11 10 09 08 07 06

Table of Contents

Gila Monsters

North Americans have always kept their distance from Gila (HEE-lah) monsters. People once believed these lizards had poisonous breath. They also thought Gila monsters would bite and not let go until thunder clapped. Neither is true. Gila monsters do have **venomous**, painful bites. But these shy, slow-moving lizards only bite people who bother them.

Like all other lizards, the Gila monster is a reptile. Reptiles have scales, are born from eggs, and are **cold-blooded.**

◀ Adult Gila monsters can weigh 5 pounds (2 kilograms). They are the largest lizards found in the United States.

What Gila Monsters Look Like

Gila monsters have hard skin. Their skin pattern is made of black, orange, pink, and yellow scales. The scales look like tiny beads.

A Gila monster stays low to the ground. Four short legs stick out from its body. A thick, fat tail drags along the ground. A Gila monster's body sways back and forth when it crawls.

◀ A Gila monster's small, black eyes blend in with its face. Its skin is bumpy and rough.

Gila Monster Range Map

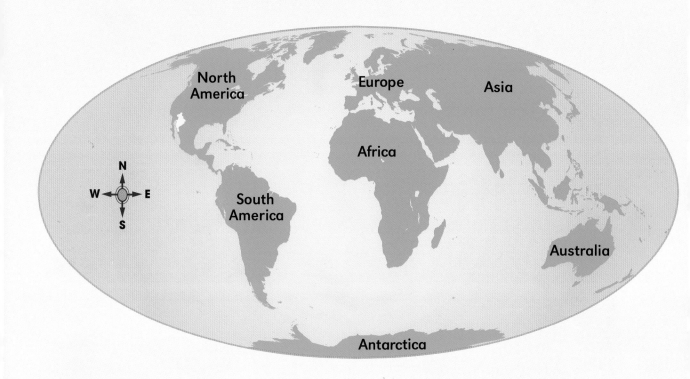

Where Gila Monsters Live

Gila Monsters in the World

Gila monsters got their name from Arizona's Gila River. Gila monsters still live in Arizona, as well as in other parts of the southwestern United States. Nevada, Utah, New Mexico, and California are all home to these lizards.

Gila monsters also live in Mexico with their cousins, Mexican beaded lizards. Gila monsters and Mexican beaded lizards are the world's only venomous lizards.

Gila Monster Habitats

Bright sun heats up the sandy desert. Gila monsters avoid the heat by spending most of their time underground in **burrows**. Gila monsters make burrows in desert hills and valleys.

Gila monsters dig burrows with their strong, curved claws. In the dry climate, these lizards make their burrows in the wet sand under desert plants. Gila monsters **hibernate** in burrows during winter.

◀ During the little time spent outside of its burrow, this Gila monster crawls across the hot Sonoran Desert.

What Gila Monsters Eat

Gila monsters find food with their long tongues. They follow animal scents by tasting the ground. One of Gila monsters' favorite foods is bird eggs. Gila monsters also eat mice, birds, lizards, and rabbits. Gila monsters swallow their **prey** whole.

Gila monsters eat huge meals. They may eat only 3 to 4 meals during an entire year. These meals must provide all their energy for months. Between meals, Gila monsters store extra fat in their tails.

◀ Usually a night hunter, this hungry Gila monster risks the hot day temperatures to grab a mouse.

The Life Cycle of a Gila Monster

Egg

Adult male
and female

Hatchling

2-year-old
Gila monster

Producing Young

Gila monsters **mate** in the spring. To get a female's attention, a Gila monster male raises his body. Two males may fight to mate with a female. They can wrestle for hours before one male gives up.

After mating, the female Gila monster digs a burrow. She lays 3 to 12 eggs in the burrow, covers them, and leaves. The next spring, baby Gila monsters hatch out of the eggs.

16

Growing Up

Gila monster hatchlings crawl around at night to avoid being eaten by birds. Hatchlings are only 4 to 6 inches (10 to 15 centimeters) long. But **predators** could easily see their black, white, and bright yellow skin during the day.

As hatchlings get older, they grow and change color. After about two years, Gila monsters are 1 to 2 feet (30 to 60 centimeters) long. Their bright yellow color gets darker, turning orange and pink. Darker colors help them blend in with their habitat.

◀ Gila monsters use a special egg tooth to slice through the eggs' leathery shells.

Dangers to Gila Monsters

Many predators eat Gila monsters. Hawks, eagles, and owls swoop down to catch them. On the ground, coyotes search for the lizards.

Humans also harm Gila monsters. Some people kill Gila monsters because they think the lizards are dangerous. People also catch Gila monsters and sell them as pets. By law, people who sell Gila monsters must have a license. The small number of Gila monsters left must be protected.

◀ Hungry birds sometimes sit on top of cactuses and search the ground for Gila monsters.

Amazing Facts

- Gila monsters can live off the fat in their tails for months.
- Gila monster nests are well hidden. No one has ever found a Gila monster nest in the wild.
- A Gila monster's bite is not venomous enough to kill a healthy person.
- Some scientists believe Gila monster venom may someday treat Alzheimer's disease and diabetes.

◀ Healthy Gila monsters, like this one, have thick tails filled with fat.

Glossary

burrow (BUR-oh)—a tunnel or hole in the ground made or used by an animal

cold-blooded (KOHLD-BLUHD-id)—having a body temperature that is the same as the surroundings; all reptiles are cold-blooded

hibernate (HYE-bur-nate)—to spend winter in a deep sleep

mate (MAYT)—to join together to produce young

predator (PRED-uh-tur)—an animal that hunts other animals for food

prey (PRAY)—an animal hunted by another animal for food

venomous (VEN-uh-muhss)—having or producing a poison called venom

Read More

Miller, Jake. *The Gila Monster.* The Lizard Library. New York: PowerKids Press, 2003.

Simon, Seymour. *Animals Nobody Loves.* New York: SeaStar Books, 2001.

Internet Sites

FactHound offers a safe, fun way to find Internet sites related to this book. All of the sites on FactHound have been researched by our staff.

Here's how:

1. Visit *www.facthound.com*
2. Type in this special code **073685424X** for age-appropriate sites. Or enter a search word related to this book for a more general search.
3. Click on the **Fetch It** button.

FactHound will fetch the best sites for you!

Index